Under the "L"

2002-3 NMI
MISSION EDUCATION RESOURCES

❋ ❋ ❋

READING BOOKS

ADVENTURE WITH GOD
The Jeanine van Beek Story
by Helen Temple

HANDS FOR THE HARVEST
Laborers for the Lord in the Far East
by A. Brent Cobb

JOURNEY TO JERUSALEM
Making a Difference in the Middle East
by Pat Stockett Johnston

MOZAMBIQUE MOMENTS
E-mail from the African Bush
by Douglas J. Perkins and Phyllis H. Perkins

TRIUMPH IN TRINIDAD
God's Promises Never Failed
by Ruth O. Saxon

UNDER THE "L"
Mission Field Chicago
by L. Wayne Hindmand

❋ ❋ ❋

ADULT MISSION EDUCATION RESOURCE BOOK

CALLED TO TEACH
Edited by Wes Eby

Under the

the

Mission
Field
Chicago

L. WAYNE HINDMAND

Nazarene Publishing House
Kansas City, Missouri

Copyright 2002
by Nazarene Publishing House

ISBN 083-411-9625

Printed in the United States of America

Editor: Wes Eby

Cover Design: Michael Walsh

10   9   8   7   6   5   4   3   2   1

To Dr. Keith Bottles,
a man of vision,
who saw the vast harvest field of Chicago
with all of its complexities
and communicated his heartthrob to his church,
this book is gratefully dedicated.

Contents

L. Wayne Hindmand, an ordained minister in the Church of the Nazarene, has pastored for 35 years on the following districts: Kansas, Kansas City, Illinois, Upstate New York, and Chicago Central. He is a graduate of Southern Nazarene University and has completed graduate work at Nazarene Theological Seminary and Olivet Nazarene University.

Rev. Hindmand is currently serving as the Central U.S.A. Region area coordinator for Stewardship Development Ministries for the Church of the Nazarene and the Sunday School chairman for the Chicago Central District. Other ministry assignments have included district advisory board, district NYI secretary, district camp coordinator, police chaplain, and finance chairperson of the Thrust to the Cities effort in Chicago.

Rev. Hindmand is married to Martha, a teacher in an inner-city public school in Chicago. They have two daughters, Julie Wiens and Janelle. The Hindmands report they are the "proud grandparents" of Jay, Joe, and Katie. They currently make their home in Oak Lawn, Illinois, a Chicago suburb.

Acknowledgments

I am grateful for the following people who took a step of faith to inaugurate and continue the Thrust to the Cities in the Chicago area:

- Dr. Bill Sullivan, director of the Church Growth Division (now USA/Canada Evangelism/Mission Department), who started the engine of faith that has resulted in an exciting chapter of missions.
- Dr. Michael Estep, then Church Extension Ministries director, for leadership in promoting thrust efforts in Chicago as well as in other cities around the world.
- Rev. Wayne Quinn, the first coordinator of the Thrust to the Cities in Chicago, who provided daily direction.
- Rev. Bob Brunson, the second coordinator, who capably led the ongoing thrust to evangelize Chicago.
- Rev. Brian Wilson, current superintendent of the Chicago Central District and former missionary, who has created new impetus for missional outreach under the "L."

I also extend my heartfelt thanks to:

- Sheila Hayes, for transcribing notes and tapes of Chicago "thrust" events.

- Martha, my beloved wife, for her insights and proofreading the text for me.
- Wes Eby, for an effective job as editor, adding color and life to the printed page.

Introduction

And Jesus went about all the cities and villages, teaching in their synagogues, and preaching the gospel of the kingdom, and healing every sickness and every disease among the people (Matthew 9:35, KJV).

God loves the cities. He must, because there are so many of them—and so many people in them. His supreme love for the world caused Him to send His Son to redeem all people. If the human race is going to be redeemed, the cities will have to sense God's power and love.

Chicago, third-largest city in the United States, is truly one of the world's great cities. Among its many landmarks is the elevated train—most often called the "L." This major mass transit system, its rails several feet above the city streets, moves thousands upon thousands of people throughout the downtown and suburbs each day. And under and around and beside the "L" live thousands upon thousands of people—longtime residents, new immigrants, grateful refugees—all part of the diverse, multicultural population of this complex metropolis.

During the last century, the world has come to America. Chicago has served as the destination and eventual home for multitudes of people who represent many and varied cultures. In the greater Chicago area alone are around a million Spanish-speaking people, 100,000 Russians, 60,000 Filipinos, 40,000 Chinese, 60,000 Asian-Indians, 35,000 Koreans, and around 25,000 of Arabic ancestry. Although these are the largest cultural groups, many more reflect the world's diversity in this megalopolis.

Who is able for such a task as this? Who can communicate with the teeming masses who speak Tower-of-Babel languages? Who can reach the vast number of people under the "L"? The answer is obvious: only men and women anointed by God and with a passion in their hearts for the lost will be effective in reaching others with the Good News.

In 1985 the 21st General Assembly of the Church of the Nazarene and denominational leaders took a huge step of faith in an effort to reach the cities of the world. It was called "Thrust to the Cities" with Chicago as the first target. Bill Sullivan, director of the Church Growth Division (now USA/ Canada Mission/Evangelism Department), became the point person to give major direction to the effort of reaching the urban dweller with the wonderful story of Jesus Christ.

At first the task seemed overwhelming. The demands and logistics appeared daunting and formidable. Without the power of the Holy Spirit, there was no way the church could reach and evangelize masses of people with so little money and so little experience. The first-century Church was a small band of Christians who tackled their world—cities and all— and turned it upside down. They made a profound difference on human history. The Church of the Nazarene believed it could happen again.

Keith Bottles, then Chicago Central District superintendent, shepherded the program and all the men and women who volunteered to be a part of the new dream. Wayne Quinn became the first coordinator of the Chicago "thrust." A year later, Robert "Bob" Brunson assumed the responsibility.

I want to share with you some amazing and exciting stories that are guaranteed to touch your hearts and increase your faith. These accounts are about the men and women God has called from other parts of the world to help build His kingdom in Chicago. Their stories read almost like biblical epics. God guided and directed these individuals in miraculous ways. What they have done has been achieved with tremendous sacrifice, and with God's help has brought about life-changing results—under the "L."

1
From Russia with Music

Praise the LORD with the harp; make music to him on the ten-stringed lyre. Sing to him a new song; play skillfully, and shout for joy (Ps. 33:2-3).

A Russian—bearded, broad-shouldered, imposing —and his wife—dainty, feminine, vivacious—began to play. He ruled the electronic piano; she, the violin. Their duets immediately captivated the audience, hardly able to believe what they were hearing and seeing. The music, so different yet beautiful, charmed the hearers. These two "strangers" were a vision of God's grace.

The setting was Chicago Oak Lawn First Church of the Nazarene on a Sunday morning. This talented couple, the Antoshins*, had just been presented to the congregation as the new Russian pastor for the city. Mikhail's love of people reflected in his countenance. Carolin's flashing eyes and smile revealed her strong faith and determined spirit.

---

*A guide on pages 78-79 provides pronunciation of unfamiliar words in this book.

Where did this fascinating pair with special musical gifts come from? Here is their captivating story.

◻ ◻ ◻

Carolin was born in Maracaibo, Venezuela, to Gladys and Edgar Garaban. Although Carolin's folks were not interested in Christianity, her grandmother talked about Jesus and read the Bible to her and her sister. This spark of interest caused Carolin to visit a neighborhood church, going all by herself when only 8 years old. A short time later when the family moved to a better neighborhood that had no church, Carolin's "religious" relationship ended.

The Garabans supported their daughter in music, and her interest and skill in the violin flourished. When she graduated from high school, she entered the music conservatory in Maracaibo to continue her studies.

A friend from the Dominican Republic invited Carolin to attend an evangelical church. Although she really didn't want to go, she accepted the invitation to humor him. The warmth of the people and the spirit of the service appealed to her. Reluctance turned to acceptance. Soon, the 18-year-old embraced Christ as her Savior and received Christian baptism.

Carolin's father had encouraged his daughter from the time she was 8 to study music in another country. Since he was enamored with Communism, his recommendation was the Soviet Union, and he sought a scholarship for Carolin to enter the music program in Moscow, Russia. This process, which took four years, was successful.

Carolin anticipated this new adventure, though understanding she would be away from home and alone for a long time. Since she had been a Christian only six months, this fit in well with her desire for a more private life with God. As she traveled to and arrived in a foreign land, her only friend was her Heavenly Father.

Settling in the dormitory of the music conservatory in Moscow, Carolin began to seek out a church. "Do you know where I can find a church without saints?" she asked a couple girls in her dormitory.

"No, we've never been, but we have a friend who knows," came the reply. "Unfortunately, she has left the city for a trip."

The director badgered Carolin, declaring that Christianity was only for old people.

At long last, the "friend" returned who knew the whereabouts of the evangelical Christians and showed Carolin how to go by train. The Venezuelan teenager, transplanted in Russia, faithfully attended this house of God for over a year.

Because of Carolin's activities with Christians, the school authorities did not want her to continue her studies. They argued and fought with her. The director badgered Carolin, declaring that Christianity was only for old people. In desperation, the young woman prayed, asking God for a solution from all the harassment.

Finally, the Minister of Culture, the conservatory director, and the secretary called Carolin to a meeting. "We don't want you here," they said. "Leave now! You're not welcome at this school."

"I won't go," the brave youth declared.

For over an hour, the officials interrogated, berated, and belittled her music ability. Yet, Carolin, with uncompromising determination, refused to submit to the demands of the school. At the end of two hours, the Minister of Culture made the decision, "All right then, we will transfer you to Odessa."

Once again she was a stranger in a new city. In Odessa she began to look for a longtime friend from Mexico, and when they finally connected, Carolin rejoiced to see someone she knew.

Her friend's roommate was Mikhail Antoshin, a burly Russian from Moscow. He had attended a music school in Moscow and was now at the conservatory in Odessa.

Mikhail's introduction to Christianity had come earlier while fulfilling military obligations. He had been invited to play the piano at a restaurant, and the guitarist began talking to him about church. When this new friend invited Mikhail to attend, on a lark he decided to accept.

"What a shock it was when I arrived and found many, many people," Mikhail says. "There were 600 seats, but they were all full, and 600 more standing. And although these were good people, I simply was not interested in religion. My communist education did not leave room for any religious crutch."

Mikhail spent three years in Moscow at the music conservatory before transferring to the one in Odessa. His new roommate was a Mexican student and, interestingly enough, a friend of Carolin's. When she moved to Odessa the providence of God brought the two—no, the three—together.

This "giant" Russian was impressed by this diminutive Venezuelan girl with dark, sparkling eyes and passionate music ability. He asked her for a date, and she, in turn, invited him to church. Because of his captivation with Carolin, he kept attending with her. After a few months, he accepted Jesus Christ as Savior in April 1986. That September he received Christian baptism.

Mikhail and Carolin Antoshin

After Mikhail's conversion, the director of the Odessa conservatory wanted the musician dismissed. Somehow, Mikhail graduated, although the KGB, the Soviet secret police, could not understand how this was possible. Miraculously, the documents describing Mikhail's religious activity disappeared, evidently due to perestroika. But future education in this school was no longer possible.

Carolin and Mikhail, deeply in love, were married in Odessa in 1986. Then the young couple moved to Venezuela, she returning to her homeland. Later, he served as the chairman of the music department for the music conservatory in Venezuela.

After some time, the Antoshins decided to move to the United States, as God was placing a desire in their hearts for a change. Their destination was Chicago, although they had no Russian friends and knew no one in America.

Mikhail and Carolin landed at the Miami airport. In a publication they found an address for an inexpensive room, yet they could not find a vacancy. Standing in the terminal, looking confused, a woman approached Carolin and asked, "Are you a Christian?"

"How do you know?" Carolin responded with amazement.

"I can feel it," the stranger said. "I can feel Jesus in you. What is it you need?"

Carolin explained they were trying to find a cheap room and showed her the address.

"Oh, no, that is not a safe place to go," the woman responded. "You have to go with me to my house." The tone of voice gave little room for rejection. This Cuban Christian in America opened her home to perfect strangers—just because of Jesus.

Carolin felt it was safe to say yes, even though this was out of the ordinary. "Why would you do this? You don't even know us at all."

<hr>

**Their friend wished them good luck
and left them standing at the airport.**

<hr>

"I know it's unusual, but I have to do it," the woman replied. The Antoshins stayed with this gracious lady for four days.

But since their goal was Chicago, Mikhail and Carolin flew northward. A friend had invited them to come and stay with him. When they arrived at O'Hare International Airport, the man met them with disturbing news. "My wife did not agree for you to stay at our house, and so the plans we made are no longer available." Their friend wished them good luck and left them standing at the airport.

For several days, Mikhail and Carolin slept in different homes each night as various pastors provided a place for them to stay. To earn a little money, the new immigrants gave concerts at several churches.

One performance was held at the Ukrainian Baptist Church. While selling their cassettes, a gentlemen approached, saying, "I know you. I cannot believe you are Mikhail Antoshin from Odessa."

"How . . . how?" Mikhail questioned.

In his answer, the man began singing one of Mikhail's songs. "I went to Odessa to meet you, but found out you had left for Venezuela. Now, *I'm* in Chicago, and *you* are here too." He showed the Antoshins a video of Ukrainian groups, playing and singing Mikhail's songs.

As the Antoshins used their recorded music and visited many churches, they quickly made new friends. One of those was Pastor José Alfaro of the Chicago First Spanish Church of the Nazarene. He invited the young couple to assist with the music at his church. They shared their talent and gifts with this Nazarene congregation for over a year and a half.

One day, Mikhail talked with Rev. Alfaro. "Carolin and I feel we need a place for a Bible study for Russians."

"I agree with you completely," their pastor responded. "There are so many immigrants from Russia in greater Chicago. Why don't we check with the Nazarene church in Mount Prospect."

Their fellow Nazarenes in the Chicago suburb kindly opened their doors to this fledgling group. The 10 people who started the group had grown to 15 within four months. It was now time to begin a church. District Superintendent Keith Bottles was ready to organize his last church before retirement—the very first Russian Church of the Nazarene in America.

"Many in my home country feel guilty when they leave," Mikhail says, "but we know this is the right place, the right time, and the right work for us. We are strangers here in America, but we feel at home. We know this is God's plan for us."

Mikhail and Carolin Antoshin, joyfully using their God-given gifts of music, are reaching people for Christ under the "L."

2

From Guatemala to an Explosion

Every day they continued to meet together . . . And the LORD added to their number daily those who were being saved (Acts 2:46-47).

"Irma, we've been invited to go to Chicago," José Alfaro said, reading a letter he had just received.

"What? . . . How did this happen?" José's wife responded, astounded by this new development.

"I'm . . . I'm not sure," José commented, equally shocked at this turn of events. "This letter is from Rev. Robert Brunson, the director of the Thrust to the Cities program in Chicago. He's asking us to come and pastor a small Spanish-speaking congregation of . . . of about 20 people."

"Do you suppose this is the Lord's will?" Irma asked. "You've been feeling for some time that God has something else for you to do."

"Could be . . . could be, Irma. . . . You know I've been restless, wondering what would be next." José sat down, staring at the unexpected letter. "Yes, this may be it. We'll pray about it and see."

José Alfaro had been a successful pastor of a growing congregation in Guatemala for some time. Although he had been offered other opportunities with increased salary, these did not interest him. God seemed to be saying something different. Then José received the surprising communication from Chicago to pastor under the "L," a place God had planted in his heart already. The Alfaros accepted.

⬭

Was our coming here really God's will?
José thought more than once.

⬭

Arriving in Chicago, the Alfaros began their ministry at First Spanish Church of the Nazarene that was worshiping in the Northside Church facility. The monumental task looming before them was to develop into mature Nazarenes this little group of Christians, which had been until recently functioning as an independent evangelical group. José began by teaching the basics of Wesleyan doctrine, which he referred to as the "hard things" for his people.

Six months passed and half the congregation left, unwilling to become the people of God in the Church of the Nazarene. *Was our coming here really God's will?* José thought more than once. He admits that the first year was indeed a tough one.

Finally, in spite of the struggles and a rocky start, new people began to attend. Yet, developing leaders took time. It was six years before the load began to shift and laypeople started to assume responsibilities in the church. God's wonderful plan for First Spanish was just beginning to unfold.

The Alfaro family desperately needed larger housing. Although José and Irma had five children, they "adopted" a young man and his relative, who had come to Chicago without a place to live. Nine people crowded into cramped living quarters.

Pastor José and Irma Alfaro (center) with their family

The Alfaro's dire need was met in 1992 when Alabaster funds helped purchase the first parsonage for the church. The next year, with only $12,000 in the bank and a vision for Chicago, Pastor José stepped out by faith to purchase a church building, seating 400 to 500 people, at a cost of over $300,000. Again, Alabaster, along with the Thrust to the Cities money, came to assist in the purchase of this house of God. The congregation was running 100-150 people at this time. But just as the Lord multiplied the loaves and the fishes, He was also multiplying the ministry of the First Spanish Church —not only under the "L" but throughout the sprawling metropolitan area.

Under Pastor Alfaro's leadership a few years earlier in 1988, the church sponsored a baby congregation in Mundelein with 20 people—the first of many church plants. The Hispanic explosion had begun!

Another Spanish-speaking congregation in the southern suburb of Blue Island was begun and then organized in 1995 when Pastor Sergio Mayorga joined the Chicago team.

▭

First Spanish lost at least half its income and . . . showed a zero balance in its checking account.

▭

Another church was started in Summit in a building that had been purchased from a sister denomination. Today that church, pastored by Gilmar Pineda, is self-supporting, and the mayor of Summit has added his support to the congregation.

By this time, First Spanish had mothered three

baby churches under the "L," and each time had given of its own lifeblood. But now it was time to add another. The Highwood Spanish Church with Pastor Byron de Leon began in a house in the Highwood area. First Spanish seeded this new church with people and partnered with the district in subsidizing its beginning.

In December 1995 First Spanish took on an enormous task when the congregation gave 40 members and their families to start the Emanuel Church of the Nazarene. Rev. Pedro Aguilar, Pastor José's assistant, was appointed pastor of the new congregation. This church plant meant that First Spanish lost at least half of its income, and at the close of the assembly year showed a zero balance in its checking account.

"What are we going to do?" Shepherd Alfaro's flock asked.

"We're going to pray and trust God," the pastor responded. With hard work, sweat, and tears, the church began to grow again. In the meantime, the Emanuel Spanish Church grew to more than 125 people.

Enrique Polanco arrived from Guatemala. Two families from the suburb of West Chicago were ready to begin a Spanish-speaking church in their area. José Alfaro connected these few believers with Rev. Polanco in July 1998. This new-start church was running 35 in its first year with the district and First Spanish assisting in half of its expenses.

All this explosion resulted, in part, because Alabaster funds came to Mission Field Chicago. The acquisition of a parsonage for the Alfaros and a larg-

First Spanish Church of the Nazarene in Chicago

er church building provided the base for God to reach out into the Spanish community. But His plans were not finished yet.

In early 1996, Mikhail and Carolin Antoshin presented a gospel concert at First Spanish. Carolin from Venezuela and Mikhail from Russia performed instrumental duets that amazed and entertained, while glorifying the Lord. Shortly after the concert, Pastor Alfaro offered Mikhail and his wife the position of minister of music at First Spanish. They gladly accepted, adding energy and excitement to the church's music. This dynamic duo ignited gospel music on the scene in a fresh way. The church continued to explode.

During the next year and a half, the Antoshins

made friends with Russian immigrants. It was now time to start a Russian Church of the Nazarene in America, and once again First Spanish helped birth a baby congregation. First Russian Church located in Mount Prospect on July 1, 1997. José was not about to leave the Hispanic families in Mount Prospect without some hope, and in September 1998 he sent Mario Delgado to begin a Spanish church. For a time, three congregations met in the Mount Prospect Church of the Nazarene: the English-speaking church at 10 A.M., the Spanish-speaking church at 12 NOON, and the Russian-speaking church at 2 P.M. A fourth language service, Korean, was added later.

After assisting each new church start, First Spanish rebounded in attendance and finances. This vibrant church, which has already helped to birth eight new congregations, has plans to partner with the district and other congregations to plant more in the suburbs of Waukegan, Melrose Park, and Cicero as well as in the city limits of Chicago itself. Waukegan is presently starting a church for its Hispanic community, and a Bible study is underway in Melrose Park. Pastors are being trained, tutored, and nurtured by Pastor Alfaro and other leaders who teach in a Spanish-language district ministerial study program started in 1985. First Spanish, now overflowing its facilities with more than 400 in the morning worship service, is looking for solutions to its space problems. This "mother" church plans to continue to birth strong new babies—under the "L" and beyond.

José is a proud papa. And rightfully so.

3

From Vietnam to a Divine Call

Then I heard the voice of the LORD saying, "Whom shall I send? And who will go for us?" And I said, "Here am I. Send me!" (Isa. 6:8).

Saigon had collapsed . . . the American military were withdrawing . . . the land was destroyed . . . the Vietnamese were devastated. It was 1975, the beginning of the end of the Vietnam War.

The future looked bleak and dangerous for the family of Ngan Tran. Her physician father had been employed by the government when the family moved to Saigon. Now chaos reigned; people begged to get out of Saigon. What a frightening time!

An American businessman had rented from Ngan Tran and her mother for nine years. He bade them farewell, knowing they were a marked family. Because of Tran's kindness to him, he sought a way to get Tran and her mother out of Vietnam. After going to the airport, he returned, excited to report the two women had less than 24 hours to pack and flee with him. Ngan Tran and her mother flew to Clark

Air Base in the Philippines and finally to a small Iowa town where a sponsor befriended them.

Small in stature, humble in heart, but possessing a firm courage to try the impossible, Tran is the essence of the Vietnamese people. In America she wandered from place to place, visiting one relative or friend after another. For a time she worked with refugees, but seemingly could not find her niche.

Ngan Tran took training in radiation biology. When her chemistry teacher invited her to a church picnic, Tran heard the gospel of Jesus Christ for the first time. "Pastor, I was raised by my parents as an ancestor worshiper," Tran said. "To me, God was a supreme creator, but far away and impossible to reach. You tell me that I should worship Jesus Christ because He is God. How can I know for sure what you say is true? Can you prove it to me?"

⊏⊐

**Tears of repentance flowed
down Tran's cheeks.**

⊏⊐

The pastor gave Tran her first Bible and asked her to read it. "Jesus, if You are God," she prayed, "please reveal yourself to me." The King James Version was too difficult for this little Vietnamese lady with broken English, so she put it aside, unread. Finally she gave the Bible away.

Busy with her studies, she transferred to a university, forgetting all about her prayer. Here a friend from Nigeria gave her a Phillips translation of the Bible that was much easier to understand. Tran was about to be introduced to the Heavenly Father.

One day she came across the story of the prodigal son in Luke 15. "All of a sudden I saw myself as that person," she says. "It dawned on me that God who lives in heaven is as near to me as a father."

It was then that God showed himself to Tran, and He had been waiting for her to accept His unchanging love. "Jesus Christ, I now invite you into my heart," she prayed as tears of repentance flowed down her cheeks. "I accept You as my Savior and Lord. Please forgive me of all my faults and sins."

Now the Bible took on new meaning as she diligently began to search its pages. At the university she joined a group of international students who studied the Scriptures every Friday night. "That's when I began to grow in the Lord," she says.

One day without a job she prayed, "Oh, Heavenly Father, the communists took so many things away from us, but there are three things they cannot take away: my faith, my life, and my heart. I give them all to You. I belong completely to You."

Tran's next stop was Houston, Texas, where she obtained a job as a laboratory technician. One day a Vietnamese pastor came to speak to a group of Vietnamese Christians. "God did not bring you here to get rich," he said. "He has a purpose for each of your lives."

"I could not sleep that night," Tran says. "I prayed, 'If You want me to serve You, Lord, please show me the way.'" Tran knew that God was calling her to work among the refugees of her homeland who had come to the States.

⬭

"You must be careful in Uptown,"
the woman replied. "This is not a
safe place for you to live."

⬭

The Thrust to the Cities organizers in Chicago heard about Tran and invited her to come and be a part of starting the first Nazarene church for Vietnamese in the Windy City. When she arrived in Chicago, she knew no one. Northside Church of the Nazarene became her base and home for the first

Northside Church of the Nazarene

34

Rev. Ngan Tran with District Superintendent Brian Wilson

month. Pastor Jim Bledsoe gave her a ride to Uptown Chicago—under the "L"—to look for a place to rent and begin a church.

Tran noted that not everybody was eager to let her in. "Do you know of a place I could rent?" she finally asked one Vietnamese woman.

"You must be careful in Uptown," the woman replied. "This is not a safe place for you to live. A refugee was killed just last week."

Discouraged, Tran continued to look. "Lord," she prayed, "please give me a place to live where I can serve You."

At one building, she approached a man scrubbing the steps. "Do you know if there is an apartment available for rent?"

"How many people?" The man responded by asking another question.

"Only for me," she replied quietly with traditional Vietnamese respect.

The man's eyes lighted. "I have two bedrooms, and you can see them."

This third-floor apartment was located in the center of the Vietnamese community. Tran could visualize where the new church would be. Bob Brunson, the director of Chicago Thrust at the time, quickly rented the apartment for her, so she could begin knocking on doors and witnessing to her faith in Jesus Christ.

Tran also secured a position with the World Relief organization, and for five years she ministered to refugees. She became the caseworker for Vietnamese who came to Chicago and the conduit for the grace of Jesus Christ. Her responsibilities with World Relief included finding housing, providing food and transportation, and offering orientation and counseling as needed. As she worked with the refugees, she found many opportunities to witness for her Savior. When she presented the gospel, a number of them accepted Christ and became a part of the baby Nazarene church.

Tran's living room—under the "L"—became the

chapel for 40 to 50 Vietnamese refugees who came together each week for Sunday School and worship and for Bible study on Friday evenings. She even included time for a youth group to meet, share, and fellowship. Uptown Vietnamese Church was organized in 1988.

The Vietnamese people in Chicago, crushed and broken, found hope, faith, and joy in the heart of a little Vietnamese missionary whom God called, not to be rich in worldly goods, but to be rich in the grace and the love of the Lord Jesus Christ, and to serve Him faithfully under the "L."

4

From Jordan to Shouts of Praise

Praise the LORD. Praise, O servants of the LORD, praise the name of the LORD. Let the name of the LORD be praised, both now and forever (Ps. 113:1-2).

"Praise the Lord! Praise the Lord! Praise the Lord!" shouted Rev. Suleiman Rihani during a celebration in Chicago for all of the Thrust to the Cities churches. He was celebrating the very first Arabic church building in the United States. A new Arabic church had just been organized in Oak Lawn, and the one at Norridge had a new building—a facility specifically purchased for Arabic ministries. What an event!

Suleiman was born in Jordan to a family of farmers. The Rihani family were nominal Christians of the Greek Orthodox religion. Although Greek Orthodoxy had dominated the area since the time of Christ, the Muslim religion has now supplanted it.

In his neighborhood Suleiman grew up with a reputation as a rascal. One time as a young adult, he stole grapes from his pastor's father's home. The old gentleman tried to catch the thief, so Suleiman began to throw stones to drive him away. Not to be deterred, the elderly man hurried to his house, grabbed a gun, rushed out, and shot Suleiman in the leg. Though only a flesh wound, it captured the "thief's" attention.

The next day Suleiman returned to gain revenge by "shutting down" the church. When he arrived, however, a service was in progress, and the pastor was preaching a sermon titled "The Wages of Sin Is Death." As the minister bore down on that emphasis, Suleiman, thinking about his brush with death, was seized with great conviction. That day he repented of his sinful life and accepted Jesus as his personal Savior.

Suddenly, into view came Jalileh, the first woman to catch his eye.

For about a year, Suleiman worked as a foreman on the roads. Then the Lord grabbed his attention once again and called him into the ministry. The young adult traveled to Egypt in 1960 to study theology. After completing his training four years later, he returned to Jordan to pastor a church.

Suleiman's congregation was being sponsored by another fellowship. "The Lord gave me a building," Rev. Rihani says, "and God began to bless my ministry. Before long 200 people were attending."

But apparently because of jealousy by church leaders at Suleiman's accomplishments, he was suddenly dismissed and sent on his way without a place to serve the Lord.

Six months later, Church of the Nazarene leaders contacted Rev. Rihani and invited him to pastor a church. "The Lord again gave me another building where I could pastor," Suleiman says. From 1965-69, he labored in Amman, Jordan. During this time he decided to make a major change in his life.

Suleiman was single and needed a wife. In August 1966 a friend showed him through the community with the idea of introducing him to the "right girl." The suitor asked for a sign from the Lord: "God, may it be the first lady that I meet in the village." Suddenly, into view came Jalileh, the first woman to catch his eye. Then when he turned a different direction, she was there again. One more time he changed positions, and she came into the picture a third time.

Even though Suleiman knew that Jalileh must be the right one, he had one more sign. When he finally proposed, Jalileh did not say yes, she did not say no, she simply said, "I must pray about it." That was the exact answer the young preacher was looking for.

Before long they joined hands and hearts together in marriage and ministry. To this union five children were born: Salam, Wanies, Rami, Samih, and finally Grace. Salam gave to the family the first grandson.

Another change was a move to the United

The Rihani family. L. to r.: Samih, Grace, Suleiman, Salam with his wife, Wanies, Jalileh, and Rami.

States. "God spoke according to a voice in my heart," Suleiman says. "The thought lodged in my mind that the church in the United States has sowed evangelism in my country for years. And I was one of the fruits of that evangelism. Therefore, I should go to America to reach my people there."

Suleiman accepted a job as a translator for the consulate that assisted Arabic families traveling to the United States. At the same time, he still desired to go to America himself. God granted him the desire of his heart, for He had led Suleiman to the position of translator to serve as a stepping-stone to his longed-for destination. After some time the consulate asked him if he would like to go to America.

"Yes, I would," he responded hopefully. "But I have no one to sponsor me." He knew without a sponsor he would never see America. After hearing their translator's reply, the consulate granted him a visa to go to Chicago. God was providing a way for Suleiman to fulfill his vision of ministry.

Upon arriving in the States, Rev. Rihani started an independent Arabic church in Chicago, which soon grew to 200 people. Though this ministry was certainly a success, there were those who desired the "fruits" of Suleiman's labor. "They departed me without letting me know," he said.

General Superintendent Jerald Johnson contacted District Superintendent Bottles in regard to the Thrust to the Cities in Chicago, suggesting the name of Suleiman Rihani as a possible contact for the Arabic people. That name was passed on to Rev. Bledsoe, pastor of Chicago Northside, who opened the doors of the church to Brother Rihani. His call to Suleiman was a simple one. "We need your help. There are 80 Arabic families who need a pastor."

⊂⊃

**The celebration was explosive.
Shouts of joy rang throughout the church.**

⊂⊃

When Suleiman began his Nazarene ministry under the "L," people began to come. Before long the southside of Chicago heard about this new Arabic church on the northside. Many Arabic families lived in the south suburbs and asked Rev. Rihani to come and organize a church in their area too.

Norridge Arabic Church of the Nazarene

Suleiman contacted Pastor Hindmand of the Chicago Oak Lawn First Church to see if a facility would be made available. After discussion and prayer, both men agreed to commit their efforts in starting an Arabic church on the southside. The Chicago Oak Lawn Arabic Church of the Nazarene was organized in 1987.

The church on the northside received new facilities when a building was purchased with funds from Alabaster and the Chicago Central District. The Norridge Arabic Church, also organized in 1987, had the first church building for an Arabic Nazarene congregation in America.

What a tremendous accomplishment! The celebration was explosive. Shouts of joy rang throughout the church. When Suleiman gave his report to the district assembly, he led the people in shouting, "Praise the Lord! Praise the Lord! Praise the Lord!"

A short time later, Suleiman was instrumental in organizing another Arabic church in Windsor, Canada. In 1996 an Arabic church in the south Chicago suburb of Lansing was begun under the pastoral leadership of Hosny Reyad. Suleiman brought him to the States primarily for that responsibility. In 1999 Rev. Reyad began one more Arabic church in Tinley Park. It seems that what God has planted in the heart of one man, Suleiman Rihani, has now taken root and is expanding—under the "L."

In recent years, Rev. Rihani suffered two strokes and endured problems from diabetes. Yet, he continued to minister from his pulpit until he died in July 2001. His latest projects were translating a book in Arabic titled *The Other Israel*, which sold out shortly after it came to the market for Arabic people. He wrote a book titled *Occupations in the Bible*.

Suleiman Rihani—the patriarch from Jordan was truly the patriarch of the Nazarene Arabic work in America, serving faithfully under the "L."

5
From Jordan with Visions

*And afterward, I will pour out my Spirit on all people.
Your sons and daughters will prophesy, your old men
will dream dreams, your young men will see visions.
Even on my servants, both men and women, I will pour
out my Spirit in those days* (Joel 2:28-29).

Aha! She is coming soon! Jamil Qandah thought
in anticipation. *Surely, she must be the one for me.*

Jamil had enrolled at European Nazarene Bible
College (now European Nazarene College) in
Switzerland to continue his education. Although
studies were his first priority, he knew he needed a
life partner. He began to pray for a spouse—in
earnest. And when Jamil heard that a Finnish girl
was coming to the college, immediately he thought
she might become his wife. To this young man, the
yet-unknown woman was a vision—a dream come
true.

☐ ☐ ☐

Jamil was born in Jordan to a Catholic family,
and he served in that religious tradition as an altar
boy. His life, however, soon changed when his father,

a policeman, moved to a community with no churches. The majority of the townspeople were Muslims. During the family's five-year-stay, they encountered few Christians. Although Jamil was exposed to Islam, the language and customs didn't mean much to him. Their religious rituals and everyday practices were simply an inherited part of life for the followers of Mohammed.

When Jamil was a teenager, a traumatic accident resulted in a hip fracture and bone infection. In the next five years, he experienced 14 surgeries and spent most of his time in bed. The excruciating pain and prolonged suffering caused him to rely on the religion of his childhood. He prayed to the saints and angels for relief; yet, he hurt intensely in body and remained empty in heart. Jamil became a bitter and disillusioned young man.

"Why me?" he cried out in frustration and anger. But the heavens gave no answer.

A cruel and brutal 15-year civil war was about to explode, engulfing Lebanon and its people with panic and destruction.

After five years he was able to walk again, but only with great effort. He returned to high school and, at the same time, began working in a hospital as an elevator operator. When a friend at work invited him to a Church of the Nazarene, Jamil accepted and the Lord spoke to him during the service. All of the bitterness and anguish of the past years overwhelmed him, and he began to call out to God for help. That day Jamil became a new creature in Christ Jesus. "I felt renewed," Jamil testifies. "I was truly a new person in Christ Jesus."

Shortly after, Jamil believed God was calling him to full-time Christian service. He attended the Nazarene Bible school in Beirut, Lebanon, for two years. Suddenly, he had a strong feeling to leave the country—immediately! The timing proved to be propitious, as a cruel and brutal 15-year civil war was about to explode, engulfing the country and its people with panic and destruction.

◻ ◻ ◻

Jamil's "vision" at European Nazarene Bible College (ENBC) was Merja, who was raised in a Lutheran family in Finland. Upon graduating from high school, she attended the University of Helsinki and the Science of Sibelius Academy Conservatory where her contact with Campus Crusade for Christ in 1972 brought her to a personal faith in Jesus Christ. The morning following her conversion, she woke up cheerfully and said, "Good morning, Jesus."

Moving to a new apartment, she found herself alone, needing Christian fellowship. One day riding the Metro, she saw two men from the Salvation Army and asked them about a Bible study. One of them, going to the same location she was, exited the bus with her. He explained to Merja that on the ninth floor of her building, his brother had a Bible study every Tuesday night. He was a Nazarene who had attended European Nazarene Bible College. Her desire to go to an English-speaking Bible college, along with the leadership of the Lord, pushed her in the direction of ENBC.

In college, as Jamil daily watched for his "vision," his future wife, to arrive, he worked as a breakfast cook. But obviously his mind was not on his job. One of Jamil's duties was to boil milk. During one of his hope-filled moments, he forgot all about the milk, and it boiled over, filling the whole dining hall with a pungent odor.

Finally, the "vision" appeared. The first time Jamil was together with his wife-to-be, he was so flustered that the sugar container lid came off, and he poured the entire amount into his drink.

⊂⊃

The suitor had an ulterior motive, which included negotiation for marriage.

⊂⊃

But Jamil had a mission, and there was no time to delay. "Would you study with me in the library?" he asked.

"Yes," Merja responded.

The suitor had an ulterior motive, which included negotiation for marriage. "I'm not looking for someone to date," the young man said, getting right to the point. "I'm looking for someone to marry." He then gave her a date to consider, since he did not want to waste time on the courting process. He mentioned everything he could think of to scare her out of the possible marriage, including the prospect of living in Jordan perhaps for the rest of their lives.

Many of the professors and school leaders tried to discourage the couple's relationship, since it was a cross-cultural event, and both would need to adapt tremendously. Yet, before long they were engaged, and Jamil took his future wife to visit his family in Jordan.

"Do you want to cancel the wedding?" Jamil asked his fiancé the night before the wedding. "You can, if you are uncertain."

"Jamil, I believe God has ordained that we should marry," Merja said with conviction. "Of course I want to marry you. I have no doubts."

Because of the need for further education, Jamil had a new "vision." *What about going to America?* he thought. *In fact, why not?*

The visionary applied to Bethany Nazarene College (now Southern Nazarene University) to pursue a master's degree in public education. Soon, Jamil and Merja were on their way to the United States. Suddenly, it dawned on them that they had forgotten about housing. When they arrived after a one-day delay, Professor Snowbarger was waiting for them at the airport with a limousine to take them to their home—which, of course, they didn't have.

The couple arrived at the school with their eight suitcases and stacked them on the campus lawn. It was four o'clock in the afternoon. *Where would they live?* they wondered.

School officials asked them if they had made arrangements for housing, and the answer was no. Since Jamil and Merja arrived late, everything was full. But, wait! As providence would provide, one efficiency apartment was available.

The young couple moved in with no furniture. In addition, they needed pillows, blankets, and literally everything to set up housekeeping. When a church announced that a family who had just arrived in America needed "everything," the congregation rallied. Furniture and all the basic needs were donated. Merja had been particularly concerned about a bedspread, and even it was provided. And the furnished items were not cheap; they "shouted" quality. The

Jamil and Merja Qandah with their children.
(Standing l. to r.) Daniel, Heidi, Samuel, and Alex.

Lord's faithfulness continued throughout the Qandah's days in college, even in the small things.

During their time in Oklahoma, they attended the Britton Church of the Nazarene. Once when a missionary spoke, the message awakened a missions call in both of them. A letter to their district superintendent, a missionary application, and ordination brought them to the screening process for a specialized appointment as Nazarene missionaries. This latest "vision" took the Qandahs to Cypress to teach at the Bible college in the Middle East.

The Qandahs have four children: Alex, who was born in Oklahoma, and Samuel, Heidi, and Daniel, born in Cypress.

When Jamil and Merja's term of service (from 1985-89) at the Bible college expired, the family planned to return to Bethany for their furlough. In a contact with Rev. Rihani in Chicago, Jamil learned of the need for an Arabic pastor. Instead of going back to Oklahoma, the Qandahs arrived in Illinois—to take part in another "vision."

In January 1989 the Oak Lawn Arabic Church of the Nazarene began to function as the second Arabic church started under the "L." Jamil became a bivocational pastor with a teaching position in the Chicago public school system.

Jamil's "visions" took him from Jordan to Switzerland to find his Finnish wife, to America to obtain an education, to Cypress to serve as a Nazarene missionary, and to Chicago to pastor an Arabic church. Jamil Qandah—truly a man of vision.

6
From India to Challenges

Have I not commanded you? Be strong and courageous. Do not be terrified; do not be discouraged, for the LORD your God will be with you wherever you go (Josh. 1:9).

"God, I can't see You," Sunil spoke out in the darkness. "I can't feel You. Are You there?"

"Yes, My son. I am with you." The Voice, so real and welcomed, broke through the despair that pervaded the room.

"But, why, O God? Why haven't I been healed?" Sunil asked, not in an accusatory tone, but out of pain and frustration. The partial paralysis from a spinal injury lingered, seemingly not improving at all.

"Sunil, I am with you," the Voice responded, calming the young man's fears. "Just be patient, My son. Your life has been given to Me, and I will use you for My glory."

This unusual encounter with the Heavenly Father changed Sunil Gaikwad's focus and future. The gifted young adult had just started his college studies in Bombay, India, when he suffered an unexpected impairment, forcing him to delay his education. Now, at long last, he had hope and a purpose for living.

☐ ☐ ☐

Sunil Gaikwad is a third-generation Nazarene from Maharashtra State in central India. His life is a testimony to the faithfulness of Nazarenes and their strong belief in missions around the world.

Sunil's grandfather, Konduji Yangad, was one of the early Christian converts when the Church of the Nazarene opened mission work in this vast Asian subcontinent. Konduji, raised in a Hindu home, was a leader in his community, located in a central province of India.

To most East Indians, Christianity was considered a foreign religion, and Christian believers brought humiliation to their families and communities. But since Mr. Yangad was a community leader, he was able to overcome the pressures, opposition, and persecution that arose following his conversion to the Christian faith. Through the years, because of his faithful example and witness, he was known as the "Abraham" of the Church of the Nazarene in India.

Mr. Yangad's family was large with 11 children and a host of relatives. Prabha, one of his daughters, married Yohan Gaikwad, who came from a strong Hindu family. This union was an arranged marriage, following Indian tradition. Yohan, the only Christian from this high caste Hindu family, was led to the Lord by E. Stanley Jones, the well-known Methodist missionary of the 20th century. Because of Yohan's decision to embrace the Christian faith, his family disowned him. He had to flee for his life and give up all claims for inheritance. Later, he was introduced to the Church of the Nazarene, where he met his wife.

God blessed Yohan and Prabha with seven children, five boys and two girls. Sunil, one of their sons, was born in the Reynolds Memorial Hospital, the Nazarene hospital in India. In fact, his mother was one of the first Indian nurses at the hospital. From his infancy, Sunil was immersed in sound biblical, holiness teaching from his family, and later from attending Nazarene schools at Chikhli.

After graduation from high school, Sunil began his college career. Then, suddenly, an accident brought an abrupt end to his studies. In divine providence, God used this experience to speak to Sunil in specific ways.

After Sunil's health returned, he enrolled in a seminary near Bangalore. Graduating with a bachelor's degree in theology after four years, he returned to Bombay to become the associate pastor at his home church. During the next five years, he was involved in evangelism and church planting, helping to establish seven other churches.

For a time, Sunil was "loaned" to an indigenous missionary movement with the goal of reaching other areas of India with the gospel. Through his contact with this organization, he met Alvina, who was serving in the mission office. With a heart for God, she desired to serve Him. Before long, Sunil and Alvina fell in love, and with their parents' consent the young couple united their hearts and lives together.

Rev. and Mrs. Sunil Gaikwad and their daughter

Nazarene missionaries John and Mary Anderson had ministered to Sunil's grandparents. Indeed, John Anderson Jr. gives credit for the prayers of Sunil's grandfather, Konduji Yangad, for his own personal ministry. John Sr. and Sunil's grandfather had been prayer partners and often prayed for this MK (missionary kid), John Jr., as he grew up in India. Later, John Jr. ministered to Sunil's parents, Yohan and Prabha, and even attempted to obtain Sunil's permission to work in northern India where new churches were opening. This particular opportunity never developed, however. In one of God's special surprises, John Anderson Jr. now works with Sunil in Chicago.

Sunil and Alvina decided to emigrate to the United States to study and work among their own people. During the decision-making process, he surveyed the Asian-Indian population in America and chose Chicago for its education opportunities and for ministry openings among the large East Indian community.

⊂⊃

Today more than 20 Hindu temples are located in the Chicago area.

⊂⊃

Under the "L," Sunil has encountered many challenges—challenges that seemed daunting. For example, the population of East Indians is increasing at a phenomenal rate. Today more than 20 Hindu temples are located in the Chicago area and the largest temple outside of India is being built in a western suburb of the city.

The Church of the Nazarene has committed staff and support to help win this vast unreached populace. Sunil has been appointed chairman for the South Asian Strategy Committee by the Mission Strategy Ministry office of the Church of the Nazarene.

Sunil is applying methods used by E. Stanley Jones, which include a round-table conference and dialogue center with those of other faiths. This is a key approach in establishing contacts for evangelism and follow-through for spiritual development.

As a result of Rev. Gaikwad's leadership and the support of the district, three East Indian congregations have been started under the "L." Sunil is giving pastoral care for two mission congregations: Chicago Devon Avenue and Chicago South Asian. Dr. John Anderson Jr. pastors Chicago First East Indian.

Pastors Gaikwad and Anderson are working together in supportive ways, even though they come from different subcultures in India. It's possible within the next few years that new congregations could be birthed from groups already meeting in Palos, Lombard, Naperville, and Des Plaines.

Sunil and Alvina Gaikwad are committed to using their hospitality and love to reach a people who know extremely little about Jesus Christ. They have willingly accepted the challenge of winning East Indians to Christ—under the "L."

7

From Laos to Freedom

Salvation is found in no one else, for there is no other name under heaven given to men by which we must be saved (Acts 4:12).

A huge dragon adorned the entrance, and a decoration like a flame of fire lined the rooftop. There it stood with its bright colors of yellow, red, and white. Who would expect a Buddhist temple in Elgin, Illinois?

The Nazarene Laotian pastor in Chicago was giving a tour of the temple and introduced us to several Buddhist priests. When I asked a monk about the decorations, he replied: "Buddha had a vision of a dragon who had taken the form of man. The man asked Buddha to allow him to be a disciple. But Buddha, seeing through the disguise, said, 'You are an animal, not man. It's against the law for you to be my disciple.' The dragon then asked, 'If I cannot be your disciple, let your disciples serve under my name.' Buddha gave permission; so, the dragon symbol atop every temple is dedicated to Buddha." I found the monk's explanation most interesting and

Pastor James with a Buddhist monk

revealing, since the dragon in the Scripture is a symbol of Satan. The result, therefore, is that every Buddhist believer is unwittingly dedicated to the devil.

Inside the temple sat a large gold Buddha, staring into empty space, with sacrifices of fruit and vegetables placed on his altar. According to Buddhist tradition, Buddha has ordered no blood sacrifices, only the fruit of the ground. Shades of a 21st-century Cain-and-Abel story. Gifts for the dead were displayed nearby to be passed on in the next life.

During the tour, I learned that the first king of Laos came from Cambodia, where he had been in exile. There, King Fagnum had learned about Buddhism and accepted it. He married his queen in the neighboring country, and they returned to Laos with a new religion, infecting a whole country with a belief that accepted no gods and many ways to heaven. Buddhists recognize that Christianity is "good," but Buddhist belief closes the people's minds to Jesus as the only way to heaven. When a Laotian hears of only one God and only one means of salvation, he or she refuses to pursue the claims of Christ and instead becomes a bewildered, bedeviled person.

As I observed the ornate temple and listened to the Buddhist monks that day, I realized, in a fresh way, that Buddhism was at my doorstep, no longer confined to the Far East. And Buddhist beliefs were impacting my immediate world.

▢ ▢ ▢

J. Sisouphanh Ratthahao was raised in a Buddhist home. His mother, whose family fled China during Mao Tse-tung's regime, married a devout Buddhist. Just before the communists took over Laos, Sisouphanh's father became a Christian. Immediately, the state indoctrinated the new believer in Communism.

In 1979 the Ratthahao family fled to refugee camps in Thailand. There, Sisouphanh converted to the Christian faith and began to attend Bible studies conducted by missionaries. In the small library the missionaries provided, the young man read in the Holy Scriptures that there is no other name, except Jesus' name, whereby he could be saved.

⊂▭⊃

"I suddenly realized," Sisouphanh says, "that . . . Buddha was *dead!*"

⊂▭⊃

"I suddenly realized," Sisouphanh says, "that Jesus was divine because He rose from the dead. Buddha was *dead!* Mao was *dead!* But Jesus is *alive!* I soon vowed to emigrate to America and attend Bible school to become a minister of Jesus Christ."

The Ratthahaos moved to California in 1980, where a relative was pastoring a Laotian church. Three years later God provided a way for Sisouphanh to attend a Bible college in Minnesota. Then he returned to the West Coast for a wedding—his own. He and Mary Prung married on August 11, 1984. Two children have joined this family: Darlene in 1986 and Billy in 1989.

After Sisouphanh graduated in 1987, he moved to the Chicago area to pastor a Christian and Missionary Alliance Church (C&MA) in Aurora. A year later, he became the director for planting Laotian churches, finding this ministry most fulfilling.

Brian Wangler, pastor of the Elgin Church of the Nazarene, realized the Laotian people in his community did not have a pastor. When Brian met

Rev. Ratthahao, whose tenure with the C&MA had ended, the Nazarene pastor said, "Come over here and help us. You are needed here in Elgin."

After prayer and seeking the Lord's will, Rev. Ratthahao abandoned his plans to return to California and accepted the new assignment in Illinois. Pastor James, as he is affectionately called by his Anglo brothers and sisters, is on the staff of the Elgin Church. His children have become an integral part of the church fellowship.

Rev. and Mrs. Ratthahao with their children, Darlene and Billy

Pastor James in front of Elgin Church of the Nazarene

Pastor James has become a Nazarene pastor under the "L," moving freely among Laotian families and Buddhists monks with the message of hope and freedom.

8

From Guatemala to Victory

But thanks be to God! He gives us the victory through our Lord Jesus Christ (1 Cor. 15:57).

I have had it! Byron said to himself. *I can't take it anymore. I'll kill myself.*

Byron's depression drove him to drink again. Joining a companion, he sunk into one of his frequent binges. Then, taking his wife and son to their home for safety's sake, he drove around and around the city in an erratic, crazylike fashion, hoping to kill himself in a car wreck. Somehow, he was still afraid to take his life directly. When the suicide attempt failed, he decided to stop at a liquor store to buy more booze, longing to numb the monster that controlled him.

□ □ □

Byron's problems began many years earlier. When he was born, his parents, Javier, a shoemaker, and Sylvia de Leon, already had five older children, three girls and two boys. This latest baby, named Indalecio, became just one more mouth to feed.

The de Leon home in Guatemala was torn by strife. Alcohol was Javier's demon; therefore, his wife and children were often his target of frustration and anger. The abuse in the home created much havoc. Sylvia, in desperation, would sometimes run away and stay with relatives for a while, leaving her youngest son to fend for himself.

After a few years of the father fighting with all his children, Indalecio—who became known as Byron—was the only one still at home. Each of his older siblings left, one by one, deciding their fate would be better away from this arena of pain. The little lad survived, scrounging for himself among his neighbors and friends.

Byron's schooling started when he reached his seventh birthday, but it only lasted three months. The call of the river nearby was too much. He preferred playing with his friends down at the riverfront every day. He was nine years old before he finished the first grade.

After years of mistreatment, Sylvia divorced Javier and went to live with her brother, taking Byron with her. This environment was not much better. Byron's uncle, who owned two cantinas (bars), "hired" Byron and his mother. Bar fights broke out daily, and prostitutes slithered their way among the customers. Before long, Byron began stealing to make a little extra money.

When the lad was 10, Sylvia took him on a long journey to visit his grandmother in the high mountains. Grandmother, who lived in Santa Cruz del Quiché, was thrilled to see her family. One day when Byron was occupied, his mother slipped away, abandoning her son. When he realized what had happened, he panicked. He found himself left all alone—except for his grandmother—in a strange place. "This was perhaps the deepest hurt of my life," Byron says, "to know my own mother had left me behind."

During his three-year stay with his grandmother, she insisted he start back to school. He finally finished fourth grade.

In this mountain community, parties with homemade brew and all types of debauchery were common. Before long, young Byron joined in. These depraved affairs helped him forget his pain and feeling of rejection.

One day with no warning, his mother returned for her boy. What a happy day it was for Byron to be reunited with his mother!

Sylvia and the young teenager traveled back to Guatemala City. Right after their arrival, a devastating earthquake killed thousands of people and destroyed much of the city. The quake, opening a huge crack in Byron's bedroom, jarred him out of bed. He tried to get up several times but was thrown back to the floor again and again. Finally he and his mother made it to the door, but found it jammed. It took them 15 minutes to pry it open. Miraculously, they escaped with no injuries.

To compound all the tragedies of his life, Sylvia was now blind, and 14-year-old Byron became the responsible person for his mother. Moving back to their old home, Byron began working in the family shoemaking business.

The many adversities of Byron's young life took a heavy toll on his mind and emotions. He became an alcoholic, following in the footsteps of his father, and frequented the prostitutes of the area.

———

Making the trek across Mexico on foot, their arduous journey took a year and a half.

———

As Byron grew up and left his teen years, a lovely lady by the name of Lillian, caught his eye. Lilly, as she was known, noticed this young man as well, pleased with what she saw. Their mutual attraction resulted in a wedding. Byron, at age 20, married Lilly and began a new home. *Maybe my troubles will cease*, he thought.

Three years later, the de Leons decided to move to the United States. Making the trek across Mexico on foot, their arduous journey took a year and a half.

Arriving in Texas at long last, Byron hired on as a ranchhand for three months. Then, traveling on to Chicago, Lilly joined him five months later. They both worked in a factory, manufacturing metal strips for packaging.

A new location, unfortunately, did not change Byron. For years the couple argued and fought, hardly civil to each other. When they learned of the death of a sister-in-law, they returned to Guatemala. The shock of a close relative dying served as the catalyst for Byron to begin another drinking binge, this one lasting 31 days.

Byron began to suffer with a demon tic. At night, fearful and terrorized, he was afraid to sleep, as dark figures appeared and haunted him. Voices began to tell him to kill himself. Running from his shadow, he returned to America, but found he could not even hold a job because of his state of mind. Oppressed and tyrannized by demons, he drank even more, trying to drown out the voices that screamed inside his head.

Then came that fateful day, July 4, 1991, when Byron decided to end it all. After his unsuccessful try at suicide, he stopped to buy more alcohol. But, instead of going into a liquor store, he found himself in a White Hen Pantry supermarket!

In his confusion, Byron let slip what his plan was. A Christian man overheard and approached the troubled Guatemalan. Putting his finger in Byron's face, he said, "If you kill yourself, you will be in hell. God does not like for a man to end his life. You had better think about your family." This only caused the alcoholic's inner turmoil to intensify.

Byron sought counsel among Catholic priests he knew. "Father, I need help," Byron confessed to one priest. "Can you help me? Can God really help me?"

"You need to see a psychiatrist," was the response. Byron went home, his mind perplexed, his heart unchanged.

But God had another design for this wayward, rebellious man. One of Byron's sisters, who had moved to Chicago, had become a Nazarene. "Pastor Alfaro will give you some answers," his sister said. "He's helped many people. Let's go see him. I'll go with you." Searching for any possible solution, Byron consented.

Rev. José Alfaro, pastor of First Spanish Church of the Nazarene, did not take long to size up the miserable seeker. "You are a sinner, separated from God our Father, and you need Jesus Christ," the Nazarene pastor said with kindness in his voice. "It was the devil who tried to get you to kill yourself. Satan is the voice that is shouting inside your head."

A book that had come recently to Byron titled *How the Devil Works on People* seemed to confirm what Rev. Alfaro said. "The last step for the devil is to force you to kill yourself and destroy the image of God," the pastor continued.

**No more alcohol. No more drugs.
At 29 years of age, Byron was free at last!**

After wrestling with the devil, Byron defied the enemy and challenged, "Satan, you cannot kill me. I am in the hands of Jesus." Yet, the tormented man left the minister's house, still lacking the peace and victory he desperately desired.

"Let's go to church, Lilly," Byron said to his wife the next Sunday morning. Lillian thought he meant the Catholic Church, since that was their background. "Oh, no," he told her. "Let's go to the evangelical church."

"That's much better," Lillian replied.

As soon as Byron walked into the church, he made his way directly to the altar. "I think God is asking you to repent," Pastor Alfaro said. So, the anguished man, overcome by conviction, repented and wept throughout the entire service. For two hours he prayed and cried out to God. The struggle was intense. But, by the end of the day he was free. No more alcohol. No more drugs. At 29 years of age, Byron was free at last! Peace and victory came, flooding his heart and mind.

The new Christian began to grow in the Lord, faithfully attending church and studying God's Word. Three years later, a missionary spoke at the

Rev. Byron de Leon and his wife, Lillian, at his ordination

Rev. de Leon's congregation

church and gave an invitation, asking people to work in the harvest field. Once again, Byron fell at the altar, weeping and battling God's call. That night, he stubbornly refused to say yes.

It took another three months before he was ready to surrender. "My son, I think God is calling you to the ministry," Pastor Alfaro told him. God was, and Byron finally responded, yielding his life to the Lord's service.

In less than a month, Byron's pastor introduced him to a field of labor—a house church in Highwood, a Chicago suburb. First Spanish sent the new pastor there in 1993, while at the same time he studied for the ministry at a Nazarene school for Hispanic ministerial students. Rev. de Leon's congregation is now running 65 in attendance, and it has already birthed a second house church.

The year 2000 was a watermark one for Byron and Lillian. On June 8 they received their United States citizenship. Later that same day, Byron was ordained into the ministry of the Church of the Nazarene.

Only God could find a lad in an alcoholic home in Guatemala, save him from a demonic suicidal attempt, transform his life victoriously, mold him into a man of God, call him to the ministry, and challenge him to serve Him under the "L."

Rev. Byron de Leon—a living testimony of God's marvelous grace and glorious victory.

Epilogue

by Rev. Brian Wilson,
superintendent of Chicago Central District

"Amen," I found myself saying as I read the manuscript Rev. Larry Hindmand prepared for this book. I have come to know well and love the men and women in these stories. They are some of the finest leaders with whom God has allowed me to serve for the past four years in this urban mission under the "L."

The story of the multicultural work in Chicago continues to be written as God opens doors to new communities and to new language and culture groups. As the church obediently walks through missional doors, God is calling dynamic leaders and providing contextualized strategies that will be effective in telling the greatest story ever told—Christ's salvation, full and free! Since the writing of the manuscript, developments in these churches affirm a bright and exciting future for an inclusive, evangelical, holiness people known as Nazarenes.

Our Russian- and Ukranian-speaking church people have expressed loneliness at being the only Nazarene congregation of the sort in the United States. In response, the Chicago Central District is partnering with Pastor Mikhail and Carolin, along with Dr. Tom Nees's Office of Mission Strategy USA/Canada and other districts in North America in a church planting effort among Russian populations across the continent. Places like Sacramento, Denver, Indianapolis, New York, San Francisco, St. Louis, and others are proving to be fertile ground for Russian-language ministries. We are partnering with our missionaries in the CIS (the former Soviet Union) to provide ministerial training in the Russian language.

Pastor Ngan Tran, our Vietnamese pastor, has retired to Paris, France, but has agreed to return to Chicago from time to time to teach a class in our ministerial training program. Our theological education network in the Church of the Nazarene is truly international. Before retiring, Ngan made sure her congregation would be well cared for. Rev. Do Tran and Rev. Hoang Huynh have followed her example in responding to God's call to minister to the Vietnamese community in Chicago. The congregation now shares the facilities of the Chicago Northside Church of the Nazarene, where Rev. David Aaserud is pastor.

In July 2001, I preached at the home-going celebration for Rev. Suleiman Rihani. Having battled with physical ailments for several years, the Lord called Suleiman once again—this time to be with Him forever. This pastor's widespread influence was evident as people gathered from all over the globe to honor him—from Jordan, Egypt, Canada, and both coasts of the United States. They came from the Nazarene church as well as other church groups he had influenced. As the congregation rose to its feet in celebration of his life and ministry, we joined voices the way Suleiman had so often encouraged us to do, exclaiming "Praise the Lord! Praise the Lord! Praise the Lord!" Our Arabic churches continue to grow, and the three existing congregations are working on plans to reach the yet unreached in Chicagoland by starting at least three new works in the next 10 years.

Under the able leadership of Sunil Gaikwad and John Anderson, the South Asian work is picking up speed. A recent VBS on Devon Avenue reached 30 new families. This storefront location in the main South Asian market area in the city is showcasing the gospel of Christ in an effective manner. Our South Asian Nazarenes at Chicago First East Indian Church are planning a Work and Witness trip to India to help the victims of earthquakes and support the work of our churches in that country. Missions has come full circle as immigrants to this land catch a vision for ministry both here and in their homeland.

Pastor James and the Laotians in Elgin have merged with the English-speaking congregation to form a multicultural, multilingual church. Rev. Rodney Miller serves as senior pastor, while Pastor James is associate for Laotian Ministries. Elgin has also recently begun a Hispanic work, making this a trilingual church. Such is the shape of multicultural ministry in the years ahead.

The Hispanic or Latino population is where, without a doubt, the Church of the Nazarene is seeing the greatest harvest in terms of the numbers of people who are coming to Christ. As immigration waves change, our harvest fields also change. But for now, we thank God that the fruit of our church's mission work in Latin America has resulted in the preparation of missionaries, like José Alfaro, Sergio Mayorga, and Pedro Aguilar, who have found ways to prepare and recruit pastors like Byron de Leon, Enrique Polanco, and others. These are leading a movement of church planting among the fastest growing segment of the North American population. May their tribe increase to the honor and glory of God! The Hispanic churches in Chicago believe God is calling them to begin 30 new congregations in the next 10 years.

An update on Hispanic ministries would be incomplete without explaining a shift in the model of ministry being used to start new works among this population segment. While at times it is necessary to start a church as a single-language, non-English-speaking congregation, I have been encouraging our existing churches to embrace those of other cultures and languages as part of their own church, becoming an inclusive church. The 2000 census shows, for the first time, there is no ethnic majority in Chicago. We are a city of minorities, finding ways to live together. God's voice is being heard as He calls His church to lead the way in modeling unity in the midst of diversity.

Several of our pastors are providing leadership and developing models for this type of church. Rev. Rodney Miller, senior pastor at the Elgin Church of the Nazarene, is seeing the blessings of Laotians, English-speaking, and Spanish-speaking families fellowshipping as one church. Children who go to the same public school during the week also attend common Sunday School classes. The first generation immigrant parents of many of them, however, attend a worship service in the language of their homeland. Rev. Rick El-Talabani of the Crystal Lake Church has also begun a Spanish ministry as part of his existing English-speaking congregation. Rev. Carl Ray and the Lansing Church have started a Hispanic ministry as part of the existing congregation. Chicago First Spanish, which for years has provided translation into English, fully anticipates starting an English service soon. Now that's a first! Imagine, a Spanish-speaking church reaching out to the English-speaking people in their area. These are truly missional times.

In Chicago we are learning to move away from worship as the most segregated time of our week, and shifting toward worship as a coming together of the immigrant, the displaced, the refugee, the Native American, the third- or fourth-generation North American, and the missionary from another land. As we come together under the "L," we find that God is already there. He is already at work. What a privilege to join Him there! As we do, we are becoming one people—a people of a common faith, a common hope, a common mission.

Pronunciation Guide

The following information is provided to assist in pronouncing unfamiliar words in this book. The suggested pronunciations, though not always precise, are close approximations of the way the terms are pronounced in English.

Aguilar, Pedro	ah-gee-LAHR PAY-droh
Alfaro, Irma	ahl-FAHR-oh EER-mah
José	hoh-SAY
Antoshin, Carolin	an-TOH-sheen KARH-oh-lihn
Mikhail	meek-hie-EEL
Aaserud	AH-suh-rood
Bangalore	BANG-guh-lohr
Chikhli	CHIHK-lee
de Leon, Indalecio	day lay-OHN een-dah-LAY-see-oh
Javier	hah-vee-EHR
Delgado, Mario	del-GAH-doh MAH-ree-oh
El-Talabani	EHL tah-lah-BAH-nee
Gaikwad, Alvina	GIE-kwahd al-VEE-nah
Prabha	prahb-HAH
Sunil	soo-NEEL
Yohan	yoh-HAHN
Garaban, Edgar	gah-rah-BAHN EHD-gahr
Huynh, Hoang	WHEHN WHAHNG
Maharashtra	mah-huh-RAHSH-truh
Mao Tse-tung	MOU tseh-DOONG
Maracaibo	mahr-uh-KIE-boh
Mayorga, Sergio	mie-YOHR-gah SEHR-hee-oh
Mundelein	MUHN-duh-line
Pineda, Gilmar	pee-NAY-dah HEEL-mahr
Polanco, Enrique	poh-LAHN-koh een-REE-kay
Qandah, Jamil	KAHN-duh jah-MEEL
Merja	MEHR-zhah

Ratthahao, Sisouphanh	RAHT-tuh-hou see-soo-PAHN
Reyad, Hosny	ree-YAHD HOHZ-nee
Rihani, Suleiman	ree-HAH-nee SOO-leh-mahn
Wanies	wah-NEES
Salam	sah-LAHM
Rami	RAH-mee
Samih	SAH-mih
Jalileh	jah-LEE-lah
Santa Cruz del Quiché	SAN-tuh KROOZ del kee-CHAY
Sibelius	suh-BAY-luhs or suh-BAY-lee-uhs
Tran, Ngan	CHRAN NUN
Tran, Do	CHRAN DOH
Yangad, Konduji	YUHNG-guhd kohn-DOO-jee